INDEPENDENCE HALL

Independence Hall

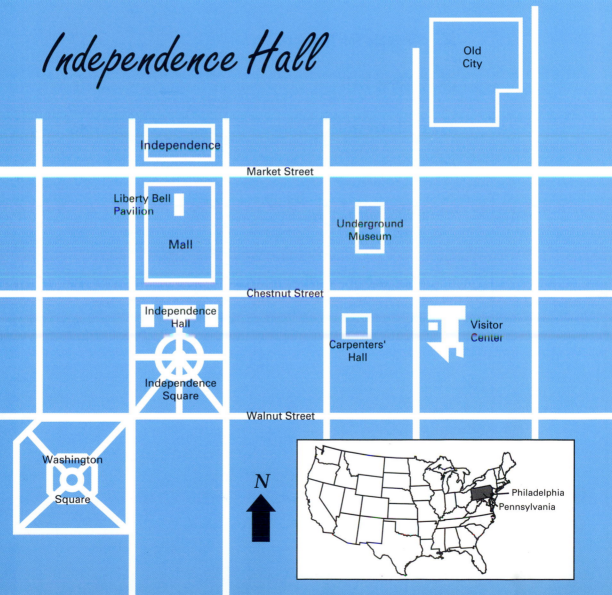

Old City

Independence

Market Street

Liberty Bell
Pavilion

Mall

Underground
Museum

Chestnut Street

Independence
Hall

Carpenters'
Hall

Visitor
Center

Independence
Square

Walnut Street

Washington

Square

N

Spruce Street

Philadelphia
Pennsylvania

CONTENTS

1. State House...7

2. Struggle for Independence...................................17

3. Liberty Bell...31

4. Philadelphia Celebrates..................................45

5. A Tour of the Park.......................................55

Independence Hall:
A Historical Time Line.......................................67

Visitor Information..70

Index...72

Photo Credits

All photos courtesy of Independence National Historical Park Collection,
except: The Penn Mutual Life Insurance Co., page 46; Sara Lee, page 53.

Library of Congress Cataloging-in-Publication Data

Steen. Susan.
     Independence Hall / by Susan Steen and Sandra Steen. — 1st ed.
        p. cm. — (Places in American history)
     Includes index.
     Summary: Describes the role this building played in the American
Revolution.
     ISBN 0-87518-603-3
     1. Independence Hall (Philadelphia, Pa.)—Juvenile literature. 2. Phila-
delphia (Pa.)—Buildings, structures, etc.—Juvenile literature. 3. Philadel-
phia (Pa.)—History—Revolution. 1775-1783—Juvenile literature. 4. United
States—Politics and government—1775-1783—Juvenile literature. [1.
Independence Hall (Philadelphia, Pa.) 2. Philadelphia (Pa.)—Buildings,
structures, etc. 3. United States—History—Revolution, 1775-1783.] I.
Title. II. Series.
F158.8.I3S74 1994
974.8'11—dc20
                                                               93-5365

Dillon Press   Maxwell Macmillan Canada, Inc.
Macmillan Publishing Company   1200 Eglinton Ave. East
866 Third Ave.   Suite 200
New York, NY 10022   Don Mills, Ontario M3C 3N1

Mcmillan Publishing Company is part of the Maxwell Communication Group
of Companies.

First Edition

Printed in the United States of America

10 9 8 7 6 5 4 3 2 1

INDEPENDENCE HALL

DILLON PRESS
New York

Maxwell Macmillan Canada
Toronto

Maxwell Macmillan International
New York Oxford Singapore Sydney

*by Sandra Steen
and Susan Steen*

CHAPTER 1

STATE HOUSE

One hot July morning, two paroled prisoners carried a covered sedan chair across the cobblestone streets of Philadelphia. They stopped at the redbrick State House. Seventy-year-old Benjamin Franklin, a representative from Pennsylvania, stepped out. He hobbled up the three steps to the front door.

In the Assembly Room Thomas McKean, a representative from Delaware, paced back and forth, watching for the door to open. McKean hoped that his fellow representative from Delaware, Caesar Rodney, had received his urgent message and would arrive in time.

Thomas Jefferson, sitting at the Virginia table, logged the morning temperature. Other

The Assembly Room, State House

representatives arrived and gathered in small groups. They argued over the same issues they had been discussing for weeks. They dared not open any windows in case someone might overhear their arguments about a crucial resolution.

A few men fanned themselves to keep cool. Others swatted horseflies that bit through their white silk stockings.

When the State House clock struck nine, John Hancock, president of the Second Continental Congress, rapped his gavel. The meeting came to order. McKean glanced at the door for Rodney. The outcome of the crucial resolution depended on Rodney's vote.

During the morning, it rained. Hancock stalled for time. He read committee reports aloud. Finally, around three o'clock, Caesar Rodney arrived. He slumped into his chair. A green scarf covered the cancer sores on his face. Rodney explained he had been delayed by thunderstorms and had ridden all night from Delaware.

Shortly after Rodney's arrival, Secretary Charles Thomson called for a vote on the resolution. When his name was announced, the exhausted Rodney stood. He knew his vote would cost him all hope of ever going to England for cancer surgery. He spoke in a clear voice: "I vote for independence."

On July 2, 1776, after all the representatives had voted, Secretary Thomson announced the unanimous vote for independence from England and the king's rule. The Assembly Room fell silent. The men knew they had just committed treason, which meant death by hanging.

The idea of a place where people could live independently in peace and with religious freedom had begun with William Penn, a member of the Quaker religion in England. In 1680 Penn asked King Charles II for payment owed to his deceased father. The king granted him a large piece of land in America. Penn put his ideas to work in the city he called Philadelphia, the Greek word for "brotherly love." By 1710 Philadelphia had become the largest city in the New World.

As governor of Pennsylvania, William Penn created a Council and Assembly that passed their own laws, while other colonies answered to

William Penn

the king. For years the Assembly held meetings in private homes where they rented rooms. In 1729 the Assembly set aside money to build a State House. Committee members argued over a plan and location.They chose Andrew Hamilton, a lawyer, to design the building.

Then in 1732 master carpenter Edmond Woolley supervised the construction of the State House. Brick masons dug up red clay from the riverbanks and made bricks for the building. They used leftover bricks to build a wall to keep out mischievous boys.

The Assembly met in the unfinished building for the first time in 1735. After the completion of the wings on both sides of the State House, the townspeople moved city documents from their homes into the east wing. Next they carried their books to the upper floor of the west wing. Here Benjamin Franklin established the first circulating library.

Philadelphians and representatives entered

the front of the State House through a double
door into a 20-foot-wide hall. Through an open
arch to the right, visitors could observe a trial in
the Supreme Court. Across the hall, behind the
closed doors of the Assembly Room, members
met in private. Upstairs in the room on the left,
the governor conducted business in his Council
Chamber. In the Long Gallery, along the front of
the State House, men waited to see the governor.
On special occasions like the king's birthday, the
gallery served as a banquet room.

Late one afternoon in the early 1750s, a
crowd of Philadelphians gathered at the State
House for a special event. They waited until
dusk, when a lamplighter appeared and leaned
his ladder against a new lamppost. The people
cheered as the lamplighter lit one lamp after
another. For the first time the lamps lit up
the street and the State House.

At times Native Americans attended peace
conferences at the State House. They lodged in

one of the wings and built their cooking fires on the floor. Fearing that Native Americans might accidentally burn down the State House, the Assembly had sheds built nearby to house them.

In 1756 war broke out in America. The French and Native Americans fought the British over land rights. With the help of the American colonists, the British won after several years of fighting. To pay for the cost of the war, King George III taxed the colonies on imported goods like sugar, paper, and playing cards. In protest the colonists refused to pay taxes or buy goods from England.

The king decided to cancel taxes on everything but tea. Angered by the tea tax, men in Massachusetts dumped newly imported tea into Boston harbor. (This rebellion became known as the famous Boston Tea Party.) To punish the colonists, the king sent British soldiers to close the port of Boston.

Because of the king's action, the Massachusetts House of Representatives asked the other colonies to send delegates to Philadelphia to discuss the unfair taxation. All the colonies except Georgia sent delegates. The men decided not to meet in the State House because the property belonged to the king. Instead, the delegates rented the first floor in nearby Carpenters' Hall, a building where master carpenters held labor meetings.

On September 5, 1774, delegates entered Carpenters' Hall and locked the doors. They formed the First Continental Congress and elected Peyton Randolph, a Virginian, as president. Before discussing their concerns, the men swore themselves to secrecy. In a united effort, they wrote a letter to the king with a list of their rights and complaints in hopes of coming to a fair agreement.

King George III refused to read the letter. He ordered British soldiers to remain in Massachusetts. To prepare for the possibility of war, Mas-

Carpenters' Hall

sachusetts formed a militia. Farmers, claiming they could be ready to fight in a minute, became known as minutemen. In April 1775, the minutemen fought British troops at Concord and Lexington. The American Revolution had begun.

CHAPTER 2

STRUGGLE FOR INDEPENDENCE

In May 1775, delegates from the 13 colonies met at the State House in Philadelphia. This Second Continental Congress chose John Hancock as president and George Washington as general of the Continental Army. Then Congress sent a letter to King George announcing its loyalty to England but expressing its right to self-government.

By the spring of 1776, colonists were still arguing about restoring peace or separating from England. At a convention in Williamsburg, Virginia, delegates chose Richard Henry Lee to present a resolution to the Congress in Philadelphia. At the State House on June 7, Lee urged the other colonies to join Virginia in declaring independence from England.

Congress debated the resolution. Nine colonies favored independence. Most delegates agreed that all 13 colonies must be united in declaring independence. Together, the colonies could ask other countries for money and military assistance. This aid would strengthen their army and help them win the war. After three days of debating, the delegates could not reach an agreement. They decided to continue the debate on July 1. Some delegates returned home to discuss the resolution with others in their colony.

Meanwhile, Congress appointed a committee to write a declaration to the king stating the reasons why the American colonies wanted to be a free nation. Member John Adams refused to write the document. He felt he was unpopular with Congress, and they might not accept his ideas. The committee considered Benjamin Franklin, but they feared he might add humor to the document. Finally, the committee chose Thomas Jefferson, the best writer, to draft the resolution.

In rented rooms near the State House, Jefferson took out paper and a quill from his portable desk. He thought about men's rights and liberty. He thought about his countrymen at war and his slaves at home. He worried about his sick wife. At times he looked at his violin case and wished he could play, but Jefferson kept writing. He wrote for hours, often scratching out words and adding new ones. Finally, after almost three weeks, Jefferson presented his draft to the committee. Franklin and Adams changed only a few words.

On July 1 the delegates returned to the State House to debate separation from England. They knew that voting for independence meant death by hanging. On July 2 each delegate cast his vote. When Caesar Rodney voted for independence, he broke the tie. Twelve colonies

finally voted for independence. New York delegates did not vote because they had not received proper instructions from home.

Early on July 3 Thomas Jefferson bathed his feet in cold water. He did this every morning to prevent catching a cold. He arrived at the State House at nine o'clock. Jefferson sat in silence while delegates argued about the contents of his declaration. John Adams defended the draft because Jefferson had a weak voice and disliked debating.

The delegates changed two major parts of the declaration. Since all the colonies profited from slave labor, the delegates crossed out the section about ending slavery. And instead of blaming the British for the colonies' poor treatment, the delegates blamed the king personally. They adjourned without finishing.

On July 4, 1776, Jefferson went shopping before going to the State House. He bought seven pairs of gloves for his wife and a thermom-

Jefferson and Franklin drafting the Declaration of Independence

eter for himself. At the State House Jefferson listened as the delegates edited his document. They corrected grammar and cut about 500 of the nearly 2,000 words.

The final draft adopted by the delegates contained a preamble, or introduction. Next came statements of self-government and basic human rights, which included "life, liberty, and the pursuit of happiness." The document also listed charges against the king and the formal declaration of independence from England.

President Hancock dipped his quill in the silver inkstand and signed the Declaration of Independence. Legend says he deliberately wrote in large bold letters, so King George could read his signature without his glasses. Secretary Thomson added his signature as a witness. Then a printer made copies of the Declaration.

On July 8, a crowd gathered in the State House yard. At noon Colonel John Nixon read the Declaration publicly for the first time. The

John Hancock signed his name to the Declaration of Independence using this inkstand.

crowd cheered and the State House bell rang for independence. George Washington and his troops listened to the reading of the Declaration in New York the next day. The troops celebrated by tearing down a statue of the king.

Three days later Congress outlined rules to govern the 13 states. These rules, called the Articles of Confederation, allowed Congress to make some laws, declare war, and make treaties with other countries. But overall, each state held more power than Congress.

On August 2, 1776, most members of Congress signed the official copy of the Declaration of Independence written on parchment, a delicate kind of paper. The men knew that by signing it they could lose their fortunes, their farms, and their lives. The delegates' names remained a secret for a few months. Then on January 18, 1777, Congress ordered copies of the document printed with all the signatures.

In the fall of 1777, during the American

Louis Glanzman's painting, The Signing of the Constitution

Revolution, the British seized the State House.
The Long Gallery became a hospital for the
wounded and a prison for American officers.
Cannons cluttered the yard. When the British
left, women scrubbed the bloodstains from the
walls and floor of the gallery.

After the war, Congress could not pay its war

Long Gallery

debts. It had no power to collect money from the states. In the summer of 1783, soldiers surrounded the State House during a meeting of Congress. They demanded their back pay. The members of Congress fled to New Jersey without paying the soldiers.

By 1787 Congress felt it could not operate successfully and survive. Under the Articles of Confederation, each state had more power than Congress. With a weak government, Congress feared another country might conquer America. In May 55 delegates, representing 12 states, met at the State House to revise the Articles. The government of Rhode Island refused to send delegates. It felt overpowered by the larger states.

This federal Constitutional Convention chose George Washington as presiding officer. To keep the sessions a secret, carpenters nailed the windows closed and guards stood outside the doors. The delegates from larger states wanted representation according to population, which would give them more votes. The smaller states wanted each state to have equal representation. For four months the delegates debated bitterly over a plan for a better government.

During the convention breaks, delegates planned speeches for future debates and wrote letters. Some visited the natural history museum to view a mastodon skeleton and Benjamin Franklin's preserved cat. Others borrowed books from the lending library, shopped, attended concerts and the theater, or raced horses.

The delegates at the convention finally reached a compromise. They wrote a new plan, which they called the Constitution. The government would have three branches: the executive, the legislative, and the judiciary. Congress would have two houses. The House of Representatives would consist of members from each state according to population. The Senate would have two senators from each state. This

Congress could establish a post office, print the same money for all the states, and make laws.

The delegates granted different powers to the other branches, the Supreme Court and the president, who would be elected by the people. This system of government ensured a balance of powers, so no branch could become more powerful than the others.

Historians credit James Madison, a Virginia delegate, as the father of the Constitution. Robert Morris, a Pennsylvania delegate, edited the final draft. The delegates signed the Constitution on September 17, 1787. Within nine months, nine of the 13 states approved it. On March 4, 1789, the people elected George Washington president of the United States.

In 1790 Congress moved to the county courthouse west of the State House. The Supreme Court met in City Hall, to the east. Meanwhile, construction of federal buildings began in Washington, D.C. The Pennsylvania

The back of Independence Hall

state government met in the State House until
1799. Then it moved to its new location in
Lancaster. At the beginning of the 19th century,
the State House stood vacant.

CHAPTER 3

LIBERTY BELL

In September 1752, a crowd gathered on the State House lawn. They pushed forward to admire the new 2,000-pound State House bell, hanging from a temporary frame. Everyone waited to hear the first ring.

The bellringer pulled back the bell's clapper and swung it. *Bong! Bong! Clunk!*

The crowd gasped when the brim of the bell cracked.

Years earlier, the state Assembly had chosen a bell as the symbol to celebrate the 50th anniversary of William Penn's Charter of Liberties and Privileges. This 1701 charter ensured many basic rights to Philadelphians. The most important privilege granted religious freedom, which

The bell's first note is struck.

no other colony at the time permitted.

Isaac Norris, speaker of the Assembly, had ordered the bell from England's Whitechapel Foundry in 1751. It cost $280. Norris chose a Bible verse to be engraved on the bell. He shortened it to read: "Proclaim Liberty throughout all the Land unto all the inhabitants thereof. Levit. XXV. 10."

When the bell cracked, the state Assembly

decided to send it back to England. When the members contacted the ship's captain, he said the ship was full. The Assembly did not want to wait a year for a new bell. They hired local ironworkers John Pass and John Stow to recast the bell.

Historians believe these men had never before made a bell this size. Pass and Stow may have referred to a French encyclopedia for help. In the pit of Stow's foundry, they made a mold of the bell. Then they smashed the cracked bell. After melting a few pieces, they discovered the bell had contained too much tin, which made it brittle. As Pass and Stow recast the bell, they added more copper to make the new bell stronger. When officials heard the new bell, they did not like the sound, but they agreed to keep it.

In April 1753, Edmond Woolley, carpenter of the State House, and his men raised the bell into the tower of the building. For the celebration Woolley ordered 40 pounds of beef, 36 loaves of bread, 300 limes for punch, musicians, and other items. When the bellringer struck the bell, it made a loud *bonk*. The crowd laughed and teased Pass and Stow.

Embarrassed, the men worked day and night for nearly seven weeks to recast the bell a second time. This time they added more tin to improve the sound. When they engraved the word "Pennsylvania" on the bell, they spelled it with one "n" instead of two. They also printed "LIBERTY," "ASSEMBLY," and "PENSYLVANIA" slightly larger than the rest of the words.

Without ceremony, workers hung this bell in the State House tower. Those present thought the ringing sounded better.

Meanwhile, Norris had ordered a second bell from Whitechapel. It arrived in the spring of 1754. The Assembly thought it didn't sound any better than the Pass and Stow bell. The members voted to hang the Whitechapel bell in the clock tower of the State House, where it tolled the hours.

The inscription on the bell

The Pass and Stow bell, hanging in the State House tower, rang to announce Assembly meetings. The constant ringing annoyed Philadelphians who lived nearby. In 1772 these citizens wrote a petition. Some "families had been affected with sickness," they said, and the sound was "extremely dangerous and may prove fatal." The Assembly ignored the petition. Instead it ordered the steeple rebuilt because the vibrations from the ringing had damaged the structure.

Over the next 20 years, the State House bell summoned the public to hear important news and called Assembly members to meetings. Tardy and absent members paid fines, which were donated to a Pennsylvania hospital. The bell rang when George III became king and when the French and Indian wars ended. It rang to protest the king's taxation. In April 1775 the bell announced the first battles against British soldiers at the start of the American Revolution.

At noon on Monday, July 8, 1776, the State

The clock tower

House bell rang after the official reading of the
Declaration of Independence. On July 4, a year
later, it rang to celebrate the first anniversary of
independence.

When British troops marched toward
Philadelphia in 1777, the townspeople feared
their city bells, including the State House bell,

would be melted down and used for musket balls and cannons. Workmen removed the bells from the steeples and loaded them onto farmers' wagons late at night. They hid the bells under straw, potato sacks, and baskets.

Legend says farmer John Jacob Mickley smuggled the State House bell in his wagon. He joined hundreds of soldiers, farmers, and others fleeing Philadelphia. Mickley's wagon broke down 50 miles away from the city. Several men transferred the bell onto Frederick Leaser's wagon. He delivered the valuable cargo to Zion Reformed Church in Northampton (present-day Allentown), Pennsylvania. The Reverend Abraham Blumer helped lower the bell into the church's basement.

A year later the city bells returned to Philadelphia. Then in 1781 workmen tore down the rotted State House steeple. They mounted the State House bell in the lower part of the tower. Here it pealed for the end of the war with

England and George Washington's victorious return to Philadelphia.

During the following years, the State House bell rang for joyous and solemn events. In 1787 teams of bellringers took turns sounding the bell, announcing the adoption of the Constitution. To mourn the death of President Washington in 1799, bellringers wrapped the clapper in leather to muffle the sound.

The bell rang continuously on July 4, 1826, to celebrate the 50th anniversary of independence. On that very day, unknown to Philadelphians, Thomas Jefferson and John Adams died within hours of each other. Three weeks later the bell tolled to mourn their deaths.

In 1839 an antislavery group chose a bell as a symbol of freedom for slaves. A drawing that looked like the State House bell appeared on their booklet titled "The Liberty Bell." From then on, the State House bell became known as the Liberty Bell.

Most historians believe the bell cracked on July 8, 1835, as it tolled the death of Supreme Court Chief Justice John Marshall. For the next ten years, the bell hung in silence. In 1846 workmen repaired the bell for Washington's birthday. They filed the crack's edges to prevent additional damage. Ironworkers cast the filings into small hand bells and gave them away.

During the celebration the bell rang loud and clear. By noon, however, bellringers discovered the crack had spread. The Liberty Bell had struck its final note.

After the Centennial in 1876, to celebrate 100 years of independence, the Liberty Bell gained in popularity. Between 1885 and 1915 it traveled 20,000 miles on a decorated flatcar. As it journeyed to expositions around the United States, people gathered along railroad tracks to catch sight of the famous Liberty Bell.

In 1915 Philadelphia's City Council opposed sending the bell to San Francisco, fearing the crack might lengthen. They changed their minds after 200,000 California children signed a petition asking to see the bell. The City Council decided this would be the Liberty Bell's final trip.

On February 11, 1915, the bell took part in a major first. William Ball, chief of the Bureau of City Property, tapped the rim of the bell three times with a wooden mallet. Its sound traveled over telephone wires from Philadelphia to San Francisco. At the same time in Washington, D.C., Alexander Graham Bell, the inventor of the telephone, listened to this first long-distance call.

For more than 100 years, visitors viewed the Liberty Bell at Independence Hall. For a while, the bell stood on a 13-sided pedestal with an eagle perched on top. Then it hung from a 13-link chain. A glass case protected the bell for eight years. When people complained they couldn't touch the Liberty Bell, however, workers removed the glass.

In preparation for the 200th anniversary of

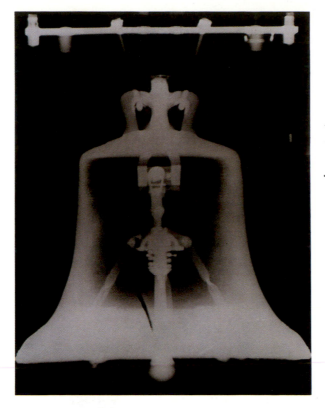

An X ray of the Liberty Bell showing its famous crack

the Declaration of Independence in 1976, the city of Philadelphia authorized a new building for the Liberty Bell. Kodak film engineers offered to X-ray the bell to see if it was strong enough to be moved. To protect people from radiation, six tons of concrete blocks surrounded Independence Hall.

On November 24-25, 1975, gamma rays passed through the bell onto a large sheet of film placed behind the bell. This process took seven and a half hours. The X-ray photograph showed minor cracks near the top of the bell and in the

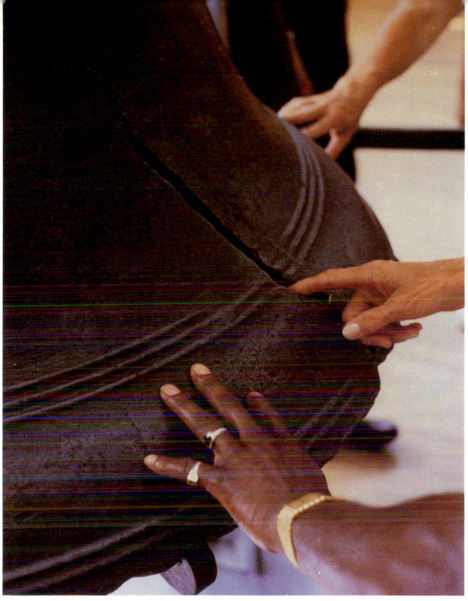

People come from all over the world just to touch the Liberty Bell.

clapper. After evaluating all the facts, the engineers approved moving the bell to a new location.

    At 12:01 A.M. on January 1, 1976, the Liberty Bell was moved to a glass pavilion across the street from Independence Hall.

In 1983 a mysterious white powder appeared on the bell. For a year experts tried to determine the source of the powder. They thought maybe air pollution or fertilizers used around the building had corroded the bell. In 1984 art conservator Andrew Lins and his staff carefully removed the powder from the bell. The source of the powder still remains a mystery.

Every Fourth of July at two o'clock, Eastern time, bells around the United States ring for four minutes. In Philadelphia, descendants of the signers of the Declaration of Independence tap the Liberty Bell in celebration of Independence Day.

Today people from all over the world visit the Liberty Bell. This silent bell symbolizes freedom for everyone. People touch and photograph the bell. Some even kiss it. Many people cry when they see the bell. Once a visitor left a rose in the crack.

CHAPTER 4

PHILADELPHIA CELEBRATES

On January 9, 1793, a crowd gathered outside the prison behind the State House. People bought tickets and pushed their way into the prison yard. Others climbed trees, rooftops, and lampposts. Thousands came to watch the first hydrogen balloon flight in America.

Cannons boomed. The crowd cheered as the band began to play. French aeronaut Jean-Pierre Blanchard inspected his yellow silk balloon. President George Washington presented him with a passport letter. It explained that Mr. Blanchard spoke French and needed help to return to Philadelphia.

The State House clock struck ten o'clock. Blanchard climbed into the basket under the

The launch of Blanchard's balloon

balloon and joined his passenger, a little black
dog. He waved his banner, with the United
States flag on one side and the French flag on
the other. President Washington, Vice President
Adams, and Secretary of State Jefferson watched
the balloon float over the State House.

The balloon traveled at a speed of 25 miles
an hour. A mile up, Blanchard took his pulse,

filled some bottles with air, and weighed a stone. He recorded his observations, sipped wine, and shared his bread with the dog.

After 45 minutes, Blanchard's balloon landed in a field in New Jersey. Frightened farmers pointed guns at him. He called out in French, but no one understood. Two men on horseback finally rescued Blanchard. One read the president's letter aloud. Then everyone understood. They helped Blanchard load the balloon into a wagon. The 15-mile trip to Philadelphia took six hours. That evening Blanchard presented President Washington with the banner from the flight.

In 1799 the Pennsylvania government moved to Lancaster, leaving the State House empty. Three years later Charles Willson Peale, a scientist and inventor who operated a museum, moved his growing collection into the Long Gallery of the State House. Visitors paid 25 cents to view mounted birds, insects, sea creatures, and reptiles displayed in natural surroundings. The skeleton of a mastodon, which Peale had discovered in New York State, became a major attraction.

Occasionally Peale used the Assembly Room to paint portraits of famous men of the American Revolution. He hung them in the Long Gallery. Peale also improved the State House grounds by planting trees and adding benches.

In order to finance a new capitol building in Harrisburg, the Pennsylvania Legislature decided to sell the State House for $150,000. However, Philadelphia had the first option to buy it. In 1816 the state Legislature accepted the city's offer of $70,000.

Eight years later, French General Lafayette, who had assisted Washington during the American Revolution, revisited Philadelphia. His carriage passed under a specially made triumphal arch, covered with canvas painted like stone.

Lafayette attended a reception in his honor

at the State House. Red and blue star-studded drapes decorated the Assembly Room.

Lafayette's visit inspired patriotism, which led to the city's decision to rebuild the State House steeple in 1828. They chose William Strickland's design with four clock faces and ordered John Wilbank to cast a large bell.

Two years later the city hired an architect to restore the Assembly Room. For the next 20 years it served as a reception room for famous visitors and presidents of the United States. The historic events that had occurred here to bring about American independence influenced the decision in 1852 to change the name of the State House to Independence Hall.

Abraham Lincoln spoke at Independence Hall in 1861 on his way to his presidential inauguration. A bronze plaque on the pavement marks the spot. After Lincoln's assassination in 1865, his body lay in state in the Assembly Room for mourners to view.

In 1876 the Independence Hall restoration committee prepared for the centennial anniversary, which would celebrate 100 years of independence. It acquired some original State House furniture and the silver inkstand used in the signing of the Declaration of Independence. Workmen moved the Liberty Bell from the Assembly Room into the hallway for better viewing. For the Fourth of July celebration, wealthy Philadelphian Henry Seybert donated a new clock and bell.

On July 4, 1876, Richard Henry Lee, a grandson of the Virginian who had proposed independence in 1776, read the Declaration of Independence to a crowd at Independence Hall. Susan B. Anthony, a supporter of women's rights, interrupted the program by handing out copies of her "Women's Declaration of Rights" to a surprised audience. Even after 100 years of independence, women, African Americans, and Native Americans had few rights.

During the next 60 years, Independence Hall underwent more restorations. In the early 1940s historical preservation groups recommended to Congress that Independence Hall become a national historical site. Congress passed a law in 1948 designating a three-city-block area as Independence National Historic Park.

Although Philadelphia owns Independence Hall, the city gave the National Park Service permission to run it. In 1950 the Park Service bought land and buildings in the historical area. Over the years, cranes tore down more than 100 offices, banks, stores, and houses in the vicinity.

Historians researched documents, diaries, and 18th-century drawings for accurate information. They studied fabrics, landscapes, and building styles of the 1770s. This information helped workers re-create the interior and exterior of the park's buildings. The reconstruction took years, and cost millions of dollars, obtained from private donors and the U.S. government.

For the 200th anniversary of the Declaration of Independence in 1976, the National Park Service planned huge celebrations. In order to accommodate the millions of expected visitors, a Visitor Center, Liberty Bell Pavilion, and museum at Benjamin Franklin Court were built. On June 26, 1976, Freedom Week began with the Great Bicentennial Balloon Race. Fourteen hot-air balloons followed the route of America's first manned balloon flight of 1793, re-creating French aeronaut Jean-Pierre Blanchard's flight over the State House.

The kitchens of Sara Lee in Illinois donated a 50-foot chocolate cake, the height of a six-story building. The company shipped the cake's sections to Philadelphia in refrigerated trucks. Bakers assembled the eight tiers and frosted them in red, white, and blue icing. They placed more than 100 symbols of American history around the cake, which weighed 40,000 pounds and cost $250,000. After two days on display in

The 1976 Bicentennial birthday cake

Memorial Hall at Fairmount Park, the official cake-cutting ceremony took place during the afternoon of July 4. Visitors ate samples, and numerous charities received portions of the cake as gifts.

During the day visitors enjoyed spectacular parades and fireworks. About 25,000 people gathered behind Independence Hall to hear President Gerald Ford's speech.

At the Visitor Center on July 6, Queen Elizabeth II of England dedicated the Bicentennial Bell, a gift from her country to the United States. She read its inscription, "Let Freedom Ring!" Earlier in the day the queen received a miniature Liberty Bell made of filings from the original.

In honor of the Constitution's 200th anniversary in 1987, the National Park Service built a fountain across from Liberty Bell Pavilion. Most of the 50 states sent rocks or boulders to form the fountain's wall.

On September 17 of that year, visitors joined Philadelphians to celebrate with picnics, fireworks, festivals, rock concerts, cheese steaks, and soft pretzels. A huge parade passed by Independence Hall, and President Ronald Reagan addressed the nation.

CHAPTER 5

A Tour of the Park

Admission to Independence National Historical Park is free. Start your trip at the Visitor Center, the only modern building in the park. First watch the film *Independence.* It shows how the colonists struggled for freedom and shaped the future of the United States.

As you leave the theater, look for the stuffed eagle by the entrance. It was alive when George Washington was president. In 1855 this stuffed eagle perched on top of the State House bell.

At the Visitor Center, park rangers answer questions and suggest sights to visit. Pick up a free walking-tour map of the park and information on current events.

Outside the main entrance stands the

130-foot tower with the Bicentennial Bell. The bell rings twice a day. Next to the tower, notice the three-dimensional scale models of some of the park's buildings. These models have Braille captions to aid the visually impaired. Close your eyes and touch them.

Next head for the Liberty Bell Pavilion, the glass-walled building. Inside, a park ranger will discuss the bell's history and size. In the past the bell rang to call men to meetings and bring people together to hear important news. Today the bell doesn't ring, but it brings people together from all over the world.

Run your fingers along the crack and look under the bell at the three-foot two-inch clapper. From the glass wall behind the bell, you can see Independence Hall across the street. At night visitors may view the bell from outside through the lighted glass and listen to a taped version of the bell's history.

The most impressive building in the park is

Independence Hall, with its magnificent tower and clocks. A marble statue of George Washington, paid for by Philadelphia schoolchildren in 1860, stands in front of the building. Search the pavement for the plaques where Presidents Abraham Lincoln and John F. Kennedy gave speeches.

Pass through the reconstructed arches to the back of Independence Hall. Today the yard, with its trees and benches, looks like a park. In 1776 weeds covered the yard, and dead animals and animal waste littered the streets leading to the State House. Delegates had to watch where they stepped.

Your tour begins in the East Wing. A park ranger gives a brief history of Independence Hall. He or she might say it was built in 1732, the year Washington was born. The ranger will talk about the Declaration of Independence and the Constitution. You'll see Louis Glanzman's painting *The Signing of the Constitution.* The

Park Service commissioned him to paint it for the 1987 Bicentennial.

Inside Independence Hall, the ranger leads your group into the restored State Supreme Court Chamber. During the 18th century, townspeople often watched trials here. Only white male property owners over age 21 could serve on the jury. The accused did not sit at the table with their lawyers. Instead, they stood in the middle of the room inside the enclosed area that looks like a cage. Today we use the term "stand trial" because in the past the accused actually stood during the trials.

Look for the small boxes on the floor. During trials these boxes, filled with hot coals, warmed the feet of court officials.

Much of early American history took place across the hall in the Assembly Room. The signing of the Declaration of Independence and the Constitution took place there. Today the room is furnished with antiques and reproductions.

The State Supreme Court Chamber

Historians believe the British destroyed most of the original furniture in 1777. The original silver inkstand sits on the president's desk. Count the tables, one table for each of the 13 original colonies. Look for Thomas Jefferson's walking stick on one of the tables. Caesar Rodney's quill sits on the Delaware table.

Look at the chair behind the president's desk. A half sun is carved at the top. During the heated debates of the Constitutional Convention, Benjamin Franklin stared at the chair. He thought about the rising and setting of the sun. He compared the sun to the rising and falling of a new nation. At the close of the convention, Franklin remarked, "I have the happiness to know that it is a rising not a setting sun."

On the second floor, the ranger explains the past uses of the Long Gallery, a 100-foot-long room. It served as a museum, prison, and hospital. After a banquet, servants would remove the tables to make room for dancing. At the end of

the gallery stands a harpsichord, a pianolike
instrument. You may get a chance to hear its
tinny sound.

Next view the Governor's Council Chamber.
A portrait of William Penn hangs on the wall. If
you look closely at the floor in this room, you'll
see some original floorboards. Across the hall,
peer into the small Committee Room, once used
as an arsenal. It displays a collection of guns
and muskets.

After your tour, walk to Congress Hall, west
of Independence Hall. Congress met here from
1790 to 1800. On the first floor, you can sit on the
circular benches and listen to a ranger share
information about the House of Representatives.
You might hear the story about two representatives who started a fistfight during a heated
argument.

Upstairs in the Senate Chambers, look at the
ceiling for the painting of the eagle and 15 stars,
done around 1792. Rangers will tell you that

The Governor's Council Chamber

about three-fourths of the chairs are originals.
As they talk about the huge carpet, notice the
circular design in the center with 13 state shields,
olive branches, and other patriotic symbols.

In Congress Hall, the first ten amendments,
called the Bill of Rights, were added to the

Constitution. Here George Washington was sworn in for his second term as president and John Adams for his first. In addition, Congress established a navy, the first national bank, and the U.S. Mint to make coins.

Walk two blocks to the restored Carpenters' Hall, with its white pillars on either side of the entrance. The First Continental Congress met here in 1774.

In 1798 the Bank of Pennsylvania leased Carpenters' Hall. A bank employee and a Carpenters' Company member committed the first great bank robbery in the United States. They stole $162,821.61. The bank directors accused the blacksmith, who had made the vault key. Although innocent, he spent three months in jail. Finally, one of the robbers confessed and then disappeared. The other died of yellow fever. The blacksmith later sued the bank and received $9,000.

Take time to wander through the restored

houses along Market Street, next to Franklin Court. Reconstructed 18th-century gas lamp-posts line the street. At the print shop, you might see a demonstration of 18th-century print-ing. Drop by the post office to mail a letter. Ask the clerk to stamp it with the rubber stamp that prints Ben Franklin's "B. Free Franklin" signa-ture.

You can learn more about Franklin at the underground museum, behind the houses. Don't miss the reproduction of his sedan chair and the display of his inventions. Listen to a ranger play a song on the armonica, a reproduction of Franklin's musical instrument made of glasses filled with water. Try to guess the tune.

In the next room you can pretend to telephone famous 18th, 19th, and 20th-century Americans and Europeans and listen to what they might have thought of Franklin. Before you leave, watch the film about Franklin's life.

Afterward, head for Market and 7th streets.

A man dressed as Ben Franklin plays the armonica.

On the corner stands a narrow brick building,
the reconstructed Graff House. Visit the rooms
on the second floor, where Jefferson drafted
the Declaration of Independence. You'll see reproductions of his swivel chair and lap desk in
the parlor. In the bedroom, look for the copper
basin. Jefferson probably used one like it to
bathe his feet.

A few blocks away on Arch Street stands the Betsy Ross House. Legend says Betsy Ross sewed the first American flag here. After seeing the upholstery workroom, climb the narrow stairs to view the bedrooms.

If you have time, walk to 2nd Street near Market and visit Christ Church, with its 200-foot steeple. Sit in reconstructed pews 56 and 58, once rented by George Washington. Then search for the pews where Betsy Ross and Ben Franklin worshiped.

Independence National Historical Park offers visitors an experience of how people struggled for freedom, gained independence, and formed a structure for self-government and democracy. The events that took place at Independence Hall still affect our everyday lives. After visiting Independence National Historical Park with its 40 buildings, visitors can leave with a sense of pride in America.

INDEPENDENCE HALL:
A HISTORICAL TIME LINE

1682 William Penn founds Philadelphia.

1710 Philadelphia becomes the largest city in the New World.

1732 Construction begins on the State House building.

1752 State House bell arrives from London and cracks when rung.

1753 Pass and Stow recast the cracked bell and weeks later recast it again because of its dull sound.

1756- French and Indian War.
1763

1765 King George III taxes the colonists to pay for the war. Colonists protest the Stamp Act.

Boston Tea Party—rebellion on tea tax.

1774 First Continental Congress meets at Carpenters' Hall.

1775 Minutemen fight British troops at Concord and Lexington. American Revolution begins.

Second Continental Congress meets at the State House.

1776 July 4, Congress approves the Declaration of Independence.

July 8, State House bell is rung and Declaration of Independence read aloud at the State House.

1777 September, State House bell is removed as British troops march toward Philadelphia. Bell hidden in Allentown as General Howe seizes the State House. Long Gallery servs as hospital and prison.

1778 June, British troops leave Philadelphia.

State House bell returns to State House

1787 September 17, delegates sign the Constitution at the State House.

1789 September 25, Congress passes the Bill of Rights.

1790 State House bell tolls the death of Benjamin Franklin.

1793 January 9, first American manned balloon flight over the State House.

1799 Pennsylvania state government moves to Lancaster, leaving State House vacant. State House bell tolls death of George Washington.

1802 Charles Willson Peale opens a museum in the Long Gallery of the State House.

1816 Philadelphia buys the State House.

1824 French General Lafayette revisits the State House.

1826 July, State House bell tolls the deaths of Thomas Jefferson and John Adams.

1828 State House steeple rebuilt with four clock faces.

1834 State House bell tolls the death of General Lafayette.

1835 July 8, State House bell cracks while tolling the death of Supreme Court Chief Justice John Marshall.

1839 State House bell becomes known as Liberty Bell.

1846 February 22, believed to be the final ringing of the Liberty Bell on Washington's Birthday.

1852 State House becomes known as Independence Hall.

1860 A statue of George Washington, paid for by children, is placed in front of Independence Hall.

1861 Abraham Lincoln speaks at Independence Hall on his way to Washington, D.C., for his inauguration as president.

1865 President Lincoln's body lies in state in the Assembly Room of Independence Hall.

1876 Independence Hall restored for the centennial celebration. Liberty Bell becomes a national symbol of freedom.

1915 Liberty Bell travels to San Francisco on its final journey.

1948 Independence Hall becomes a national historic park.

1962 July 4, President John F. Kennedy speaks in front of Independence Hall.

1976 Liberty Bell is moved to pavilion across the street from Independence Hall.

President Gerald Ford speaks at bicentennial celebration at Independence Hall.

Queen Elizabeth II of England presents the Bicentennial Bell to the park.

1987 President Ronald Reagan addresses the nation during the bicentennial celebration of the Constitution.

Visitor Information
Independence Hall

General Information

Historic sites are within easy walking distance. Entrance to all buildings is free.

Visitor Center

Open 9:00 A.M. to 5:00 P.M. daily.

Offers maps and pamphlets for walking tour.

Provides theater showing *Independence* film, bookstore, and rest rooms.

Rangers give information about current special events, attractions, and activities. Limited free tickets to see Dolley Madison's middle-class home (Todd House) and Bishop White's upper-class home.

Hours

Most buildings open from 9:00 A.M. to 5:00 P.M..

Independence Hall open from 9:00 A.M. to 5:00 P.M. daily. Summer hours are longer. Entrance at East Wing by tour only. Bookstore open in West Wing.

Liberty Bell open from 9:00 A.M. to 5:00 P.M. daily. After 5:00 P.M. the bell can be seen from outside the building, and visitors may listen to a tape of its history. Rest rooms are within building.

Carpenters' Hall open from 10:00 A.M. to 4:00 P.M. Closed Mondays. Also closed Tuesdays in January and February. Closed January 1, Easter, Thanksgiving, and Christmas.

Franklin Court open from 9:00 A.M. to 5:00 P.M. daily. Rest rooms, bookstore, and theater are within the court.

Congress Hall, Graff House, Old City Hall, Second Bank (rest rooms), Todd House, Bishop White House are open 9:00 A.M. to 5:00 P.M. Closed January 1 and Christmas.

Betsy Ross House open from 9:00 A.M. to 5:00 P.M. Tuesday to Sunday. Closed January 1, Thanksgiving, and Christmas.

Christ Church open from 9:00 A.M. to 5:00 P.M. except Sunday, when hours are from 1:00 P.M. to 5:00 P.M. Closed Mondays and Tuesdays in spring. Check times with Christ Church. Guides available.

Special Events

July 4: annual Fourth of July activities

July 8: costumed dramatization of the reading of the Declaration of Independence

Additional information can be obtained from:

Visitor Center
3rd and Chestnut Streets
Philadelphia, PA 19106
(215) 597-8974
(215) 627-1776 for 24-hour recording

INDEX

Adams, John, 18, 21, 39, 46
American Revolution, 16, 25
Anthony, Susan B., 50
Articles of Confederation, 24, 27

Blanchard, Jean-Pierre, 45-47, 52
Boston Tea Party, 14
British, 14, 21, 25

Carpenters' Hall, 15
celebrations, 45-46, 51-54
Concord, 16
Congress, 24, 25, 27, 28-29
Constitution, the, 28, 58
Constitutional Convention, 27, 28
Continental Army, 17

Declaration of Independence, 18, 19, 21, 22, 24, 52, 58, 65

first circulating library, 12
First Continental Congress, 15, 63
Ford, Gerald, 54
Franklin, Benjamin, 7, 12, 64

Hamilton, Andrew, 12
Hancock, John, 9, 17, 22

independence, 10, 18, 19
Independence, 55
Independence Hall (formerly called the State House), 7, 12-14, 15, 17, 21, 22, 25, 27, 29, 30, 31, 42, 43, 44, 45, 48, 49-51, 54, 56, 58, 60-63, 66

Jefferson, Thomas, 7, 19, 21, 39, 60, 65

Kennedy, John F., 57
King Charles II, 9

King George II, 14, 15, 17, 22
King George III, 36

Lee, Richard Henry, 17
Lexington, 16
Liberty Bell (formerly called the State House bell), 31, 32, 34, 38-41, 42, 43, 44, 54, 56
    first ring/first crack, 31
    last ring/last crack, 40
    recasting of, 33, 34
    ringing of, 34, 36-37, 40
Lincoln, Abraham, 49, 57

Madison, James, 29
Marshall, John, 40
McKean, Thomas, 7, 9
minutemen, 16

Native Americans, 13-14, 50
Nixon, John, 22, 24

Penn, William, 10, 31, 61

Queen Elizabeth II, 54

Randolph, Peyton, 15
Reagan, Ronald, 54
Rodney, Caesar, 7, 9-10, 19, 60
Ross, Betsy, 66

Second Continental Congress, 9, 17
slavery, 21, 39

taxes, 14
Thomson, Charles, 9, 10, 22

Washington, George, 17, 24, 27, 29, 40, 46, 48, 62-63
Woolley, Edmond, 12